THE TURNIP PRIZE

A RETROSPECTIVE

WE KNOW IT'S CRAP...
BUT IS IT ART?

ROYSTON WEEKSZ OBE FRSA & TREVOR PRIDEAUX

CASSELL
ILLUSTRATED

CONTENTS

INTRODUCTION

The Turnip Prize is a spoof UK art award that satirizes the less well-known Turner Prize.

The prize started in 1999, when Tracey Emin's *My Bed* (1998) was nominated for the Turner Prize. Residents of Wedmore, a small village in Somerset, were astounded when the shortlist was announced and started their own competition in the belief that they would be able to produce deliberately bad yet better modern art.

The competition hinges on one crucial question: 'We know it's crap, but is it art?' Competitors submit entries of ridiculous objects posing as contemporary art, mostly made from junk and oft-titled with puns. Credit is given for entries featuring the best puns and for those displaying 'considerable lack of effort'. The winner is awarded a turnip impaled on a rusty six-inch nail.

The Turnip Prize was held at The George, Wedmore, in 1999 and 2000; in Wedmore Public Conveniences in 2001; in The Trotter, Crickham, in 2002; and has been held at The New Inn, Wedmore, since 2003. Entries for the competition are accepted from 1 November each year and the winner is announced in December. Over the years, the Turnip Prize has attracted national and international acclaim, with press coverage in Spain, Russia and the USA.

The Turner Prize is ageist as it does not allow nominations for artists over 50 years old. However, the Turnip Prize welcomes entries from all sectors of the age scale, even those sliding down the hill toward embalming.

ABOUT THE AUTHORS

Trevor Prideaux
Founder and judge, Turnip Prize

Trevor was born in Lynton, north Devon, the youngest son with eight siblings. He was thrown out of Sunday School at the age of nine for refusing to sing 'All Things Bright and Beautiful' when it was pissing it down outside. Trevor moved to Wedmore Somerset, in 1995. He is the founder the Turnip Prize and various other events in the village. Trevor lives with his partner Amanda and has a son, Radford.

Royston Weeksz OBE FRSA
Critic, TV personality, aesthete

Royston Weeksz was born in Dagenham, Essex and ran away as quickly as possible. He attended the Slade School of Art and in 1966 became Director of the Pretentious Gallery, Soho. He teaches at the New Cross Academy for Dubious Talent and has been a noted TV art critic since the early 1980s, presenting acclaimed series including *Splat! How to Comprehend Incomprehensible Art* (1986) and *All Balls – A Critic's Guide to Contemporary Art Criticism* (1993).

THE
ENTRIES

2012 LIMPETS

BY RINGS OF STEEL

2011, SEASHELLS, WOOD

One hesitates to use the term 'seashore art' (which always conjures badly executed images of brain-damaged donkeys and seagulls, painted in what appears to be their own faeces) but a cursory glance at this 2011 entry initially confirmed this critic's worst fears. The wood panel is of the type tossed overboard by horny-handed seafarers and subsequently harvested and employed by shudder-inducing 'folk artists' in all sorts of cack-handed ways. The empty limpet shells are not 2012 in number, but a mere 61. In almost all ways, this is a highly insignificant piece and really not worthy of such a significant art competition as the Turnip.

And yet, the one aspect of the piece that I feel has outstanding artistic merit is that which has been hitherto overlooked by all other commentators. It is, of course, the date. Cast your mind back to 2012, and the global event that took place that year. Or, rather, didn't take place, for the Mayan prophecy that predicted the end of the world on 21 December 2012 proved to be a rather embarrassing flop. In *2012 Limpets*, our artist makes explicit reference to this fallacious prophecy. The limpets are the fools who cling on to the belief that Armageddon will surely occur, and the number 61 of course refers to the classic Bob Dylan album *Highway 61 Revisited*. On this album is the track 'Like a Rolling Stone' with its mocking refrain, 'How does it feel / to be on your own?' – surely a reference to the aforementioned idiots who believed that the End Time was coming.

That this work was completed and submitted to the judging panel in November 2011, well before the planet's appointment with destruction, highlights the bravery and maturity of the artist. Would that more creatives showed such noble qualities!

Judge's comment:
'Limpets across the finish line.'

TURNIP RATING:

A PAIR OF NUMBER PLATES

BY UNKNOWN

2015, PLASTIC, PAPER

In *A Pair of Number Plates* two adjacent (disposable!) polystyrene plates are anointed with apparently random numbers. But these are not mere plates. And nor are these mere numbers. In an obvious commentary on the male obsession with female breasts, the unknown artist argues that size holds no relative sway. With the scattered numbers proclaiming a dizzying variety of bust measurements, *A Pair of Number Plates* sends a stern message to the fixated male psyche: 'I could be a 44F or a 30AA. Take me as I am: breast size is irrelevant.'

In *Gabrielle d'Estrées and One of Her Sisters* (artist unknown, 1594) Henry IV of France's mistress sits in a bath, stoically enduring her sister pinching her right nipple, while in the dimly lit background a female labours over needle and thread. Separated by more than five hundred years, the parallels between these two works are remarkable.

At least the 16th-century version contained some notion of beauty, albeit that it was subsumed by the social mores of the French court. *Plus ça change*, as our Continental neighbours might say. The 21st-century version, however, sees the female form reduced to mere figures on a platter; a more cutting and insouciant example of verisimilitude pertaining to modern sexual politics we would struggle to find.

Judge's comment:
'This artist clearly learned their trade plating by numbers.'

TURNIP RATING:

A ROLL IN THE HAY

BY IMOGEN CREES

2015, STRAW, BREAD

References to sexual love are embedded in Western art, but – I insist – less evidently prior to the Renaissance. Why? The flowering of the 16th-century European mind unleashed a cornucopia of highly charged, sexualized imagery; artists devoured and exploited these new, liberating freedoms.

A direct parabola can, and will, be traced from the implosive dynamic of sexualized post-Renaissance painting to 2015 Turnip Prize finalist Imogen Crees's *A Roll in the Hay*. The title is proclaimed on a strip of paper in a pleasingly ironic typeface; a bread roll (representing the staple food of life) lies nestled on a 'bed' of hay; the plastic photo of hay is in shocking contrast to the real article. And hay *is* central to this space. Mattresses (upon or around which the large bulk of human sexual activity has been enacted) were, traditionally, stuffed with it. Crees is effectively stating: 'Make hay while the sun shines. Make it here. With or without a roll. *Your choice.*'

There's a glancing nod to Pieter Bruegel The Elder's *The Harvesters* (1565), but Crees's exquisitely coded pick 'n' mix work – which all too obviously references the ultimately exhausting nature of prolonged sex – was explicitly signposted in Constable's *The Hay Wain* (1821). Under a broad, unseeing Suffolk sky, a horse-drawn wooden cart (importantly, the cart is empty) creaks arthritically through a shallow stream as the wheels 'roll' through the waters below. The desolate, angry body language of the behatted pointing figure semaphores extreme sexual frustration, just as the relaxed posture of the driver teasing his whip assumes the familiar vernacular of post-coital *ennui*. Bliss.

The brevity of this critique forbids roving cross-media to explore Crees's subtler references to Proust's *À la recherche du temps perdu*. In *A Roll in the Hay* the many tributaries of sexualized Western art conjoin into a mighty torrent. A masterpiece.

Judge's comment:
'Hay, you call that art?'

TURNIP RATING: 🐀🐀🐀🐀🐀

AMERICAN PIONEER

BY UNKNOWN

2010, PORK, PASTRY, PAPER

Feared, revered and reviled in equal measure, the national flag of the United States has been harnessed by a variety of 20th- and 21st-century artists as a totemic, postmodernist and often highly subversive examination of the American Century and beyond. Andy Warhol, Jasper Johns and guitarist Jimi Hendrix spring to mind; possibly there are others, but perhaps in this much-spied-upon era, they're keeping quiet.

The spirit of insurrection is carried forward by this shocking multi-media piece from 2010's show. The artist is anonymous, and wisely so, for this is a work that encapsulates and exposes the paranoiac historicity of the nation and its relationship to the rest of the world. The pig's ear is highly redolent of the seething mess of insecurity lying just beneath America's gleaming façade. The pie, too, is a representation of the average American's limited worldview – or, if you will, his *Weltanschauung*. 'Far better to stay comfortably within this crust', the pie's contents appear to be saying, 'than to engage with the outside world and be bitten.'

Atop these remnants of mangled animal sits the American flag: once a symbol of hope, freedom and fraternity, now nothing more than a cheap, ragged decoration attached to a cocktail stick. There is no triumphalism here. Indeed, *American Pioneer* is a deeply ironic title, given the insidious, corn-fed consumerism that rampages across the United States and wilful, woeful ignorance of the plight of others (in this case, pigs) who dare to get in the way of the proverbial capitalist juggernaut. Whatever pioneering spirit there was has been ambushed by such values; if anyone was listening to America, the work suggests, they're not any more. Because they're missing an ear.

Judge's comment:
'They've made a right pig's ear of this.'

TURNIP RATING:

ARAB SPRING

BY ASIF

2012, METAL, CLOTH, PLASTICS

The Thiepval Memorial, Somme. *The Motherland Calls*, Volgograd. The Cenotaph, London. And now, the memorial to the failure of the Arab Spring, Wedmore. To conclude this paragraph, all I can say is, 'Gosh.'

Rarely has a public-art competition of the Turnip Prize's calibre seen such a monumental, poignant and truly heartbreaking work as Asif's 2012 mixed-media entry, *Arab Spring*. Words are barely adequate here; a poor pen as mine is hardly able to describe the aching beauty, nobility and, yes, humility of the coming together of sunglasses, tea towel and industrial spring. Ordinary, piecemeal objects converge violently in a pell-mell of soaring emotions, unrestrained optimism and, finally, oceanic lows felt across the world when the Spring itself eventually collapsed under the weight of its own surge.

There is a saying in Arabic that goes thus: 'If it was going to rain, we would have seen the clouds by now'. When I gaze upon *Arab Spring*, in all its hopeless glory, I am reminded of the phrase, uttered to me by a toothless Egyptian tour guide watching from the shadows of the Great Pyramid as I searched in vain for the furled umbrella I'd left in the hotel. Fortunately, didn't rain, and so the old soothsayer's timeless prophecy proved correct. And so it is with *Arab Spring*. Where there is rainfall today, one day there may be sun. And vice versa.

Today I have emailed the Mayor of London and recommended that this fitting tribute to revolutions that went crackers be displayed on the Fourth Plinth in Trafalgar Square. Indeed, were Horatio Nelson himself asked his opinion on the merits of my campaign, I'm sure he'd respond with an approving wink of his good eye. He, too, was something of a flawed warrior.

Judge's comment:
'Asif certainly knows how to sheikh his booty.'

TURNIP RATING:

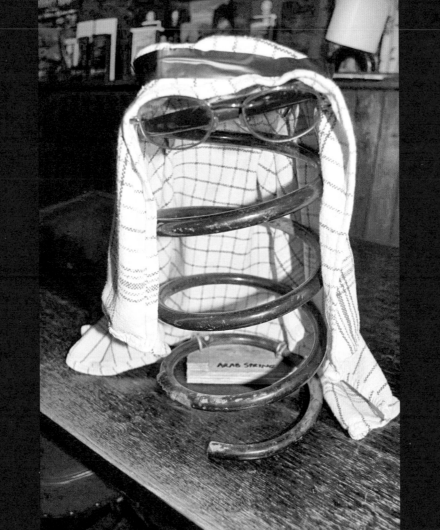

BREAD IN CAPTIVITY

BY JAMES STANDEN

2012, BREAD, PLASTIC, METAL

James Standen is an artist internationally known for his stunning and often controversial installations, which clamour for vegetable rights and world peace. *Bread in Captivity* is the latest in a long line of such works including *Peas Off* (1978), *The Grape Escape* (1984) and *Lettuce In* (1997).

This piece, created from a workaday loaf of bread and a cat's box, harks back to the Renaissance fad for scenes of often brutal enslavement, designed both to repel and titillate in equal measure. The iconography of captured loaf, subdued and subjugated, yet sentient, not knowing where it will be taken, nor indeed, from whence it came, is contrasted sharply with the harsh impartiality of the cage, its faceless parallel bars creating a deep sense of unease and foreboding.

It is significant that soon after Standen entered this work, one of the judges (quite possibly Trevor Prideaux, though we must not jump to conclusions) was seen to open the cage, remove the loaf, rend it asunder, wipe margarine upon its surfaces and divide the pieces among those gathered for the announcement of 2012's winning entry. His behaviour, though despicable within the context of this particular work, could be seen as somewhat biblical; the sharing of bread among the poor and starving of Wedmore village has undoubted Christ-like overtones. Nevertheless it was a desecration of an important work by a challenging artist, and it is to be hoped that mere judges will in future desist from interfering in the artistic train of thought and subsequent creative process.

Judge's comment:
'Tastes far better than it looks.'

TURNIP RATING:

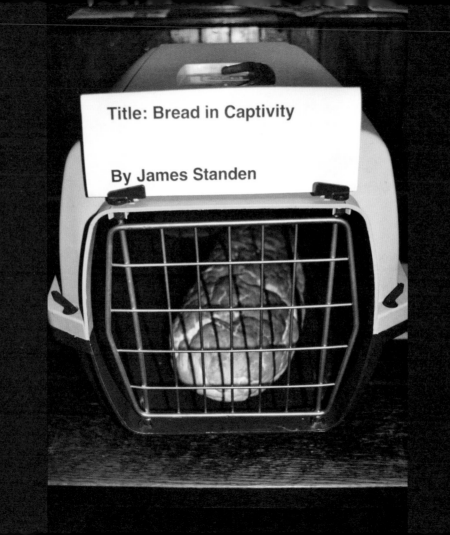

BREAST IN PLANT

BY MIKE ATKINSON

2014, PLASTIC

'My concern', said Renoir, 'has always been to paint nudes as if they were some splendid fruit.' Indeed, and it is also said that the nude does not simply represent the body, but also relates it, by analogy, to all structures that have become part of our imaginative experience.

Renoir's 'concern' is echoed quite overtly in *Breast in Plant* from 2014's competition. What are these 'fruits', if not splendid, indolent globes of sumptuous summer corpulence, lazily dangling from sagging, groaning branches, just waiting to be handled, pulled and finally plucked for consumption? Excuse me for a moment...

Ah, that's better. Where were we? Yes, indeed, *Breast in Plant* is a glorious statement of licentiousness; a libidinous, lustful look at form and function both in human and vegetable states. However, I also detect a note of subtle complexity here, for does not this image also echo René Magritte's *Le Viol* (1934), a disturbing, reductionist depiction of Woman as mere breasts and genitalia? The proximity of mammary gland to foliage hints at the full female form, and yet there are also thin strands of quintessentially British lavatorial wit here, as best depicted in the saucy seaside postcards of Donald McGill (1875–1962).

As one might suspect, *Breast in Plant* caused something of a stir when it was first exhibited, with several critics demanding its removal from the show on the grounds of obscenity. This punitive, prudish reaction is, of course, nonsense. Indeed, having obtained a substantial grant, this piquant work is now in my private collection, and I find myself constantly musing over its myriad meanings on a daily basis as I carefully trim its bush.

Judge's comment:
'It's all gone tits up.'

TURNIP RATING:

BRIEF ENCOUNTER

BY SARAH QUICK

2010, COTTON, PLASTIC, METAL, WOOD

I imagined him holding me in his arms. I imagined being with him in all sorts of glamorous circumstances. It was one of those absurd fantasies, just like one has when one is a girl being wooed and married by the idea of one's dreams.

So says the lovelorn Laura Jesson, played so wonderfully by Celia Johnson in the classic 1945 film *Brief Encounter*. And, oh! Were such sublime restraint the order of the day today! Alas, the age when romance was satisfyingly guilt-ridden and manfully repressed has long gone. I have, on occasion, walked through Green Park en route to the Royal Academy of Arts and witnessed the awful spectacle of couples practically rutting in every scrap of foliage. A swift thrust into the bush with my cane usually does the job, but the memories linger on.

There is a deep irony at work in *Brief Encounter*, Sarah Quick's biting response to the issue of post-feminist sexuality. The use of the film's title, juxtaposed with the abacus and a nasty-looking set of undergarments, points not to sober, unemotional flirtation but quick fornication and gratification, as if on a by-the-hour tariff. The position of the beads on the abacus appears to suggest that the pants-wearer has not been the first and only recipient of sexual favours that day. Indeed, by my reckoning, it looks as though some 22 others have already, and disgracefully, 'been there'.

Far from being an 'absurd fantasy', this *Brief Encounter* is a cutting comment on the tawdry, 'selfie'-obsessed world of youthful (and perhaps not-so-youthful, given my nocturnal ramblings through Green Park) fumbling. Sarah Quick's approach is nothing less than didactic, and a salutary lesson for those who approach the making of love with such ragged impertinence.

Judge's comment:
'Pants. Literally.'

TURNIP RATING:

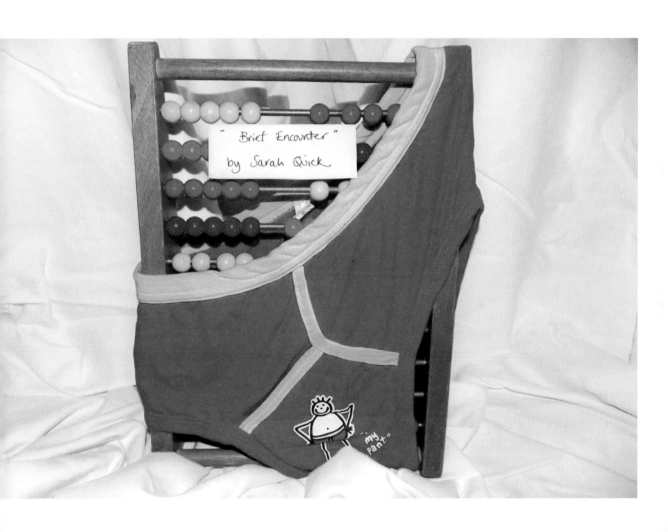

" Brief Encounter "
by Sarah Quick

CASH COW

BY SU DONIM

2015, MOULDED PLASTIC, STICKY TAPE, METAL

At the time of writing, Britain's relationship with the continent of Europe is fraught and fractious, a theme explored in this intriguing work by prominent Anglo-Swiss artist Su Donim.

Subtle use of hidden rhyming ('cash' and *'vache'*, the French for 'cow'), the harnessing of the cow as a symbol of the strife that appears to follow the European Union's Common Agricultural Policy and, of course, the disparate coinage representing internal strife between Euro-affiliated nations, all add up to the sum total of a highly cerebral piece that provokes even as it entertains.

One is reminded of Beckett's *Waiting for Godot* (1952) and the character of Lucky, an enslaved being who appears to serve no other purpose than to be tethered to the indignities of human frailty. And, yet, is Lucky 'lucky' because he's lucky enough to be told what to do and therefore has a purpose in what is otherwise a rudderless play? The question is one I feel being explored by Donim in *Cash Cow*. 'Who are we?' she asks. 'Where is this outdated, post-war project taking us? Will we have enough "milk" for the journey, and the right currency?

Will anyone buy our wares when we arrive?' Pertinent questions that only an artist of Donim's calibre can posit.

Certainly there is a fluency of interconnectedness between Donim's themes, and it may be that, diverse as they are, the wholeness of the whole is a pointer to a more harmonious future for the Continent. Artists of all ilks will no doubt appreciate this positive hint from Donim, whose ongoing and generous EU grant under the French *Money for Merde* scheme is no doubt secured for a few more years yet.

Judge's comment:
'This artist is certainly milking her small quota of talent.'

TURNIP RATING:

CHILDREN IN MEAD

BY AUNT SPONGE

2011, GLASS, ALCOHOL, CHILDREN

British folk art has, since its early beginnings, existed solely on the margins of the Art Establishment and for good reason: most of it is unadulterated balderdash, created by the mentally unwell, convicts or old people (or combinations thereof).

Recent years have seen a critical reassessment of so-called 'naive' art, with the resultant effect that a market appears to have gathered pace for dreadful daubs upon canvas, bits of grubby pottery and things knitted from pubic hair. Folk art is not a genre that appeals to this critic, and while one acknowledges the effect it has had upon contemporary artists, including Jeremy Deller and Grayson Perry, one approaches analytical appraisal with a metaphorical pomander under one's nose.

Children in Mead is a good example of the kind of British naive-school work influenced by pre-Christian myth and neo-pagan leanings towards the strangely esoteric. It was said of the Druids that their mead-making ceremonies often included human sacrifice to honour the bees, a theme that appears to be echoed here. The hand-crafted dolls smiling eerily even as the pickling process begins hint at the kind of society from which modern folk artists spring: theirs is a world of rough cider brewed in run-down barns, illegal car-boot sales, neglected infants, drug-fuelled partner-swapping on the edges of disused airfields and rotten teeth. How do I know all this? Isn't it obvious? The clues are in the subtext of every single piece of folk art in existence.

In future years, I would urge the Turnip Prize organizers not to besmirch their fine reputation by including abominations like *Children in Mead*. The sooner one discourages so-called 'artists' from evaluating their home-schooled or care-centre-encouraged efforts as high art, the better. Let's keep these people right where they feel most at home – at the very edge of civilization.

Judge's comment:
''Sss delishioussh... hic!'

TURNIP RATING:

CHILLY PEPPER

BY UNKNOWN

2014, FRUIT, WOOL

Up until the end of the 19th century the portrayal of the British at home and abroad was reflective of the Age of Empire. Encouraged by the Dutch School, portraitists including Gainsborough, Reynolds and Romney captured the buccaneering mastery of this great nation in sublime and idyllic country settings. Even the Pre-Raphaelites, unusual politics and peccadilloes aside, made more than a decent fist of classical English good looks and fine breeding.

Then, around the time of the First World War, something changed. British art went from being a pleasingly exclusive thing to a rather sootier affair. The upper and middle classes who had done so much to make this nation healthy, wealthy and wise were casually tossed overboard in favour of common plebeians. Artists including Nash, Wyndham Lewis and Lowry elevated potato-faced ruffians into a kind of itinerant nobility, and it is the latter's 'Sunday-painter' style that I feel is most closely referenced in *Chilly Pepper*.

This ruddy-faced fruit, so reminiscent of the average sun-exposed vulgarian on holiday in holes such as Malaga or Benidorm, wears an expression of world-weariness and resignation that matches the drearily cheap knit of his scarf. 'I am an English pepper,' our hero appears to be saying, 'and while I ought to be out in the midday sun, my lot is to be cold, damp and down at heart.' Overall, the effect is akin to Lowry's *Head of a Man* (1938), in which the sitter faces forward, muffler around neck and eyes red-rimmed: the result of a life of philistine pursuits

Chilly Pepper, with its uncompromising 'take-it-or-leave-it' attitude, is highly redolent of the modern English person, the sort who never raises his index finger in greeting when one waves him through at a junction or has no control over his slack jaw while eating. The overall response to this piece is a collective retch for the regrettable triumph of the lowest common denominator.

Judge's comment:
'One of this year's hotter entries.'

TURNIP RATING:

"Chilly Pepper"

CHIP AND PIN

BY UNKNOWN

2013, POTATO, METAL

Pablo Picasso's seminal *Mandolin and Guitar* (1924) was a slap in the face to those critics who declared that Cubism was dead. The sheer audacity of the subject and boldness of execution rose up in the face of conservatism, daring the viewer to either appreciate his *saut joyeux* of extraordinary rendition, or stay locked in a proverbial lavatory of misinterpretation and sheer bad taste.

And so it is with *Chip and Pin,* an equally bold collusion of disparate media that, when fused, creates a kind of transversal, vessel-like carving finely nuanced with post-structural hermeticism. The chip itself stands for Man's eternal battle with Nature. 'We may boil, we may roast, we may fry,' it says, 'but in the end there is only a void; a void we must fill with a gargantuan appetite for potatoes.'

Echoes of primitivist interpretation abound in *Chip and Pin*. The seemingly nautical nature of the chip includes lines reminiscent of the dhows that sailed upon the Nile in Ancient Egypt and were left for posterity in the pyramids. The pin is, of course, the rudder that steered these craft through antique seas, a device created by Man to navigate and chart his progress through his own life and times.

This unknown artist has taken items from a populist monoculture to create a work of transient yet heartbreaking beauty. Relationships between organic and non-organic are explored, explained and allowed to sail away with dignity across an artistic horizon, where chips and pins live in disparate, yet wholly engaging, spatial harmony.

Judge's comment:
'It's hard to pin down exactly what makes this piece so awful.'

TURNIP RATING:

CORK SCREW

BY MOKSHA MASSIVE

2013, CORK, METAL

Among connoisseurs of fine wines (of whom I am one, *naturellement*), the debate around the method used to stop the bottle ('cork' cork, synthetic cork or screw cap) continues with varying degrees of vehemence. Naturally, one dismisses utterly the screw-cap lobby as a bevy of alcoholic ne'er-do-wells, red-rimmed eyes fixated on aisle four of the local supermarket. For the rest of us, the arguments that synthetic corks prevent taint and, indeed, even 'pop' at the same decibel level as our beloved bark tissue are, frankly, mendacious. The mere thought of extruding a synthetic cork from a bottle (and, in dire emergency, with one's teeth) fills this sensitive oenologist with nothing less than *horreur*.

I share these musings over a glass of 1995 Chateau Rayas (a complex nose heralding a surprisingly cheeky bouquet) while contemplating *Cork Screw*, an entry from 2014. And as this vintage flamboyantly surfs across my tongue, I begin to understand the sheer piquancy of *Cork Screw*: it is a piece that both celebrates the discerning palate and 'nails' the real cork/fake cork argument once and for all.

There is no finesse, no refinement about the bland fixing that bores its way into the cork. The bark is from a rather low-quality bottle redolent of a 'wine circle' in Humberside. No matter: artist Massive poignantly foretells the death of cork, screwed (quite literally) by an uncaring, unforgiving wine 'industry' (a term which makes one wince) that seeks only to maximize profits and pour ill-considered plonk into the roughest of mouths. Such is the sheer brutal energy of *Cork Screw* that I must now pour myself another glass, gaze into the last embers of the fire and weep softly for what has been, and may be no longer.

Judge's comment:
'Well, that's the art world screwed.'

TURNIP RATING: 🐀🐀🐀🐀🐀

COUCH POTATO

BY UNKNOWN

2013, VEGETABLE, WOOD

'The potato', wrote Kierkegaard, 'is a highly developed thing. Like life, it can only be understood backwards, but must be experienced forwards.'

Indeed, and we can only concur with the Dane that this humble, unpretentious staple of ancient and modern cuisine contains the most profound philosophical and existential properties. Its lumpy, untutored appearance in the raw holds out very few synergetic possibilities (somewhat akin to my Mixed Media class at the New Cross Academy for Dubious Talent), and yet when one considers the potato's sheer versatility and vitality *aller de l'avant* one sees that its sculptural dynamism is there to be explored, mined and – more often than not – deep fried.

Couch Potato is a work that hints thrillingly at the spatial relationship between Man and vegetable, offering the sitter the potentiality of a resting place of superficially small comfort. As with Man Ray's *Cadeau* of 1921, we are invited to either use the couch – running the risk of marked trousers – or merely to stand back and reflect upon this as an artistic *amuse-bouche*, an appetizer which hints at a greater culinary masterpiece yet to be hewn from the living vegetable.

One wonders at the possibility of science being one day quite able to genetically modify a potato so large that one could indeed craft an entire couch from it that would comfortably seat three adults. In the meantime, this work stands as a beacon of metaphorical resonance for a future where Man *becomes* vegetable.

My only niggle is the use of the word 'couch'. So very non-U. Surely Unknown should have settled on *Sofa Potato*?

Judge's comment:
'They barely got off their scabby backside to create this.'

TURNIP RATING:

DISMAL AND

BY BONKSY

2015, WOOD, INK

Great works of art inspired by similarly lauded artists resonate down the centuries of visual creativity. Consider Manet's *Olympia* (1865); the shameless, staring nude provoked howls of 'Indecency!' on its unveiling. And yet, Manet explained, its cues were taken from Titian's *Venus of Urbino*, painted some 300 years earlier, which caused far less outrage.

In recent years, the domination of pop culture in art and the requirement to subvert prevailing cultural and socio-political mores has reached its apotheosis in the graffiti work of the British artist Banksy, whose *Dismaland* pseudo-theme park/art show in the grubby resort of Weston-super-Mare became an international cultural highlight of 2015.

Dismal And, by the self-styled 'Bonksy', picks up the mantle of referential subversion, taking a mere *jus* of the progenitor's absurd reductionism to create symbolism from a symbol itself, namely the common ampersand. Bonksy plays with the *Dismaland* pun, subtly extracting two words from Banksy's one to create new spheres of reference.

The penned illustration has echoes of Munch's *The Scream* (1893), and yet *Dismal And* is not so much screaming as shrugging its shoulders and casting down an eye – at the current state of British art, perhaps? Certainly, the artist's chosen canvas – a bland offcut of wood, such as one might find in one of the more budget home-improvement stores – suggests that work by Banksy and lesser acolytes has reached a cultural nadir; the thin end of the wedge, one might say.

Judge's comment:
'This artist said, "If you set your sights on the gutter and refuse to work hard your dreams really can come true." Agreed.'

TURNIP RATING: 🐢🐢🐢🐢🐢

EGG ON ROONEY

BY UNKNOWN

2013, EGG, CARDBOARD, INK

One of the most remarkable aspects of the Turnip Prize, aside from highlighting the very best in naive talent, is its entrants' often beautiful usage of *objets trouvés*. Indeed, it may be more accurate to describe the findings as *assemblage*, echoing André Breton's 1934 definition of so-called 'ready-mades' as 'manufactured objects raised to the dignity of works of art through the choice of the artist'.

In that respect, it is highly unlikely that a collector of stature, such as a Saatchi or a Joannou, would choose to possess a small, rather common 'coaster' depicting the face of an equally small, vulgar-looking footballer. And yet, when in proximity to what we assume is a small ostrich egg, the significance of the whole takes on an elevation in line with Breton's 'dignity' and a value, both intrinsic and financial, that places it into cultured circles far beyond those who might use it for its original purpose.

Egg on Rooney also takes on a nationalistic significance. Readers will very possibly be unaware of this Rooney's sporting achievements for his country. However, the egg – which one assumes is of the Boer War period – is the giveaway. Rooney, we are told, is on a par with the great British heroes of the past, not least Robert Baden-Powell at the Relief of Mafeking. But there is melancholy here too: the fractures in the shell and the egg's positioning over one eye suggest that our hero is somehow flawed. Can his 'good' eye see the end of his playing days on the horizon, even as he takes delivery of yet another Aston Martin Vanquish? *Egg on Rooney* hints thrillingly at what may be...

Judge's comment:
'The work of an artistic egg-o-maniac.'

TURNIP RATING:

EWE-KIP

BY DRUNK EN SHEPHERD

2014, FAUX-FUR, CARDBOARD, INK

From ancient times the representation of sheep in art has taken on a significance well beyond those of mere earthly matters. One is, of course, referring to the appearance of ruminants – usually lambs – in early Christian iconography; indeed, the Bible is peppered with references to the Good Shepherd and the Lamb of God. Sheep were an important source of food and clothing, and their essentially passive nature evidently struck a chord with Jesus, as shown here by his speech in John 10:14–15:

I am the good shepherd. I know my sheep and my sheep know me – just as the Father knows me and I know the Father – and I lay down my life for the sheep.

Jesus understood the special relationship between Man and sheep and vowed publicly to die for them. Modern observers might feel this relationship is somewhat uncomfortable. It is arguable that Our Lord might have spent his 33 years on Earth a *little* more wisely, killing Romans rather than sticking up for dumb animals. Even so, sheep-fanciers across the globe pricked up their ears, flocked to the word of the Lord, and so Christianity was born.

The French-born artist Drunk En Shepherd, in her 2014 entry *Ewe-Kip*, has encapsulated the quintessential innocence and beauty of a sheep (in this case, a female) as it reposes following a day's chewing of cud. Note the crude cardboard tray upon which the creature lies; one cannot see this other than as a reference to the shoddy manger in which Jesus was born. There are echoes, too, of Damien Hirst's 1994 opus *Away from the Flock*, but I feel the latter diverts from *Ewe-Kip* in one crucial aspect: Hirst's sheep is most definitely dead (or it is an extremely competent swimmer, even in formaldehyde). In response, En Shepherd's sleeps the sleep of a creature safe from harm and suggestions of mint sauce and piquant raspberry *jus*. A worthy winner.

Judge's comment:
'Bah, bah, blah.'

TURNIP RATING:

FIRST-CLASS MALE

BY TEAM GB

2011, MOULDED PLASTIC, GUMMED PAPER

Michelangelo's *David* (1501–04) and Rodin's *The Thinker* (1902) are the twin colossi invoked in this magical creation, highlighting the beauty and sheer power of the male form. Team GB's encounter, or several encounters, with the musculature of the masculine has obviously been redemptive and life-changing.

Indeed, it is possible there has been a slight exaggeration of proportionality between body and legs, giving one the impression that perhaps the Australian singer and personality Peter Andre has been the inspiration for the work. There is also something of a resemblance between the figure's finely chiselled jaw and Andre's Antipodean ruggedness; that said, there is also a necessary banality about the face that does not distract from the body – which is certainly not the case with Mr Andre.

Cheekily, the traditional fig leaf or modest pubic covering has been replaced by a first-class UK stamp. Is the artist suggesting that a new and unbridled British male sexuality is to be exported across the globe? Or is this a jocular comment on traditional British reserve, a 'stiff upper lip' clamped firmly around the crotch area? Certainly there is movement and wit in this piece, and a necessary throughput of fluidity that strikes at the heart of male energy, raising questions about the functionality and form of bodies, and the intimate nature of fine human specimens such as Peter Andre.

Judge's comment:
'Nice to see Her Majesty around these parts.'

TURNIP RATING:

FISH FULL OF DOLLERS

BY GRANNY ABUSE

2011, CLOTH, PAPER, PLASTIC

The complex relationship between Britain and the United States, and the notion of two nations being divided by a common language, is explored in this challenging work by Granny Abuse, a worthy Turnip finalist in 2011.

From a position of real economic hegemony just a hundred years ago, the United Kingdom is now sadly reduced to a cartoon view of itself as an island full of tea-drinking stoics: tight-lipped, buttoned-up folk with few or no strong views on just about everything, including modern art.

By contrast, the sheer audacity and cheek of the United States has come to dominate the discourse around culture, politics and aesthetics. No wonder their 'fish' is stuffed full of 'dollers'. And the misspelling is significant here: back in 2011 Granny Abuse seemed presciently to suggest that if a dunderhead like Donald Trump can make significant political advances without the benefit of a brain, the door is open for other American loitersacks to march in and take over the world.

What to do? Art, of course, has its place in the battle against American faux-imperialism. Simply put, we 'do art' much better than they do. Our appreciation is finer, our creative gifts greater. One only has to take a casual flick through this book to understand that. What we lack in confidence we make up for in sheer bloody-minded doggedness. Not for us the cheap reproductions of a Warhol, a Lichtenstein or a Mapplethorpe. Our art is rent from the ancient soil of these islands and forged from the values of hard work, creative endeavour, bulldog spirit and ruthless, relentless export of our values. Never before in the field of human conflict has so much been owed by so many to so few brave artists who, by their sheer Britishness, have...

(Editor's note: This critique first appeared in Little Englander *magazine in 2013. Please ignore any further ramblings.)*

Judge's comment:
'Send me some more dollars and you'll have me hooked.'

TURNIP RATING:

FTSE UNDER THE TABLE

BY UNKNOWN

2012, PAPER

Ah! A pun ('footsie under the table'), the like of which is rarely seen at the shortlist level of the Turnip Prize. There is a reason for this; the world of high art is not one in which visual puns have had much to contribute. Serious artists have little time for comedy, wrapped up as they are in higher thoughts. It is arguable that the likes of Dalí and Warhol have occasionally dabbled in pun-like imagery, but when studied carefully we find their messages to be more childish metaphor than subtle innuendo.

So it is refreshing to see a Turnip entrant rise to this technically complex challenge and produce a work that not only makes one laugh heartily, as I did, but also appeals to the better-minded. The FTSE reference is, of course, obvious: at the heart of the piece is the eminent *Financial Times*, a publication of solidity and decency in an uncertain world. 'Footsie', on the other hand, is a game with sexual undercurrents, very often played between persons attracted to each other who prefer to keep this evident attraction secret. We cannot imagine that the married gentlemen of the City of London would ever tap their well-shod feet against those of the pretty young things who flit from bar to bar in search of wealthy targets, but I'm told it goes on.

But this, of course, is no ordinary table. It is, of course, the famous Periodic Table of Elements, the very foundation on which all chemistry is predicated. It is of little use to artists, of course, as its visual context is largely unappealing, comprising as it does a series of nauseating pastel tones (that could only have been chosen by scientists!) overlaying an array of bland, uninformative letters that apparently mean something to people who know about these things. I, thankfully, am not among that number.

Taken together, the Table and the *Financial Times* form a unique partnership. Science and commerce. Elemental forces and hard fact. And just the merest hint of saucy feet.

Judge's comment:
'This artist is a total banker.'

TURNIP RATING:

FINANCIAL

Explore key information about

Group 1 2   3 4 5 6 7

Period

21 Sc	22 Ti	23 V	24 Cr	25 Mn		
39 Y	40 Zr	41 Nb	42 Mo	43 Tc		
71 Lu	72 Hf	73 Ta	74 W	75 Re		
103 Lr	104 Rf	105 Db	106 Sg	107 Bh		

*Lanthanoids

**Actinoids

News Briefing

Fund raises its
US fund manager

Irish economic
Ireland's recovery

Reits in tax b
Real estate inves

Maersk sea cha

Toys R Us gre

Funeral halts

Obama defends trip

HUNG LIKE A DONKEY
BY PAT MCGROIN

2015, WOOD, STRING

The ox and the donkey were powerful symbols in early Christianity and, even in our post-anti-postmodern world, retain stubbornly totemic qualities. Readings from the early medieval period deem both animals highly suggestive of the conflict between Jews (the ox, considered a clean creature) and the Gentiles (the donkey, considered dirty); Jesus' only too viable presence between the two beasts was inevitably presented as a pointer to unification and peace.

In *Hung Like a Donkey*, performance artist Pat McGroin cunningly demonstrates a gorgeous *Wirtschaftsmacht* by carefully weaving together both the *Hebdomas Sancta* (Holy Week), hubris of Christ's all-too-brief entry into Jerusalem, and His ultimate, awful destiny, as fulfilled by Roman and Jewish accusers. By employing an executioner's rope, as opposed to hammer, nails and wood, McGroin highlights the plight of those who have died for their beliefs since Jesus' self-sacrifice, using the donkey to symbolize those who know their fate and accept it, yet remain as wilfully stubborn as the proverbial donkey. That McGroin chooses to elastically reference the title

of the piece within the artwork itself is only too indicative of the sign Iēsus Nazarēnus, Rēx Iūdaeōrum (INRI), that hung at the foot of the cross. McGroin has created a very Golgotha of a piece: powerful, caustically spiteful, yet all too redemptory.

It has been suggested that the phrase 'hung like a donkey' has a double entendre but, having scoured several encyclopaedias and academic publications, I can report no validation for this assertion. That said, sources in the rather narrow field of contemporary urban vernacular have hinted that the Antipodean phrase 'budgie smuggler' is something of a polarized opposite to 'hung like a donkey'. Again, no credible academic evidence can be found for this.

Judge's comment:
'Forget the donkey, this is all bull(shit).'

TURNIP RATING:

Hung like a
donkey

By
Pat McGroin

HUSHED PUPPY

BY JACK RUSSELL

2011, PLASTIC, CLOTH

There was a flurry of excitement in the judges' chambers when this entry was received just in time for the 2011 prize. Was this Koonsian piece of pointed absurdism really created by *the* Jack Russell MBE, the former Gloucestershire and England international cricketer turned painter of pleasant if undemanding works in oil and pencil?

A quick call confirmed that *Hushed Puppy* was not of the suspected provenance. Upon learning this, I suspected that the work might provoke controversy, and so it proved. A noisy demonstration outside the glittering New Inn, home of the Turnip Prize, by outraged dog owners and their aggressive pets almost derailed the 2011 ceremony, and there was some relief that the entry did not make the final cut into the top three.

However, with hindsight we can see that *Hushed Puppy* was, in a way, foretelling the very controversy that would surround the work itself and subsequent world events the following year. Russell seemed to know that his work would be discredited, and that there would be calls for it to be withdrawn. And so, more pertinently, through the work itself Russell indicated his feelings of subjugated helplessness at those freedom-of-speech campaigners silenced and imprisoned around the world. The obvious example, and the one I feel most resembles our 'hushed' pet, is Julian Assange, the founder of WikiLeaks, who voluntarily entered Ecuador's London Embassy in 2012, where he sought asylum. Assange's ongoing battle with Big Government reflects Russell's complex and metaphorical finessing; the doe-eyed dog, a label round its neck and a plastic cup shoved over its mouth, is reflective of all those in abject captivity, from Guantanamo Bay to Belmarsh Gaol. A powerful, disturbing and strange work from an artist, not a mere cricketer.

Judge's comment:
'Hopefully the last we'll hear from this artist.'

TURNIP RATING:

I CAME, I SAW, I CONKERED

BY JULINS CHEESER

2015, BIOLOGICAL MATERIAL, FRUIT, METAL, PLASTIC, RUBBER

An intriguing work, based on Julius Caesar's famous phrase (*'Veni, vidi, vici'* in Latin, for those who still appreciate that fine yet neglected tongue), which features a serrated blade, a small brown object (possibly a chestnut) and a thin, rubberized sheath, approximately nine inches long, sealed at one end and containing a featureless pale liquid that smells strongly of ripening fruit and old ale.

Artist Julins Cheeser is a noted chronicler of contemporary urban life, and it is possible that the three objects have deep interconnectedness for her at a primal, organic level. Does the chestnut symbolize the thriving of all things, only to be cut down in its prime and wrapped in man-made substances? That the whole installation is encased in plastic adds to the air of puzzle upon puzzle; was it not Winston Churchill who described the Russian nation as 'a riddle, wrapped in a mystery, inside an enigma'? He might have been describing *I Came, I Saw, I Conkered*, such is its deep penetration into the psyche, pricking the subconscious and pushing further and harder into the moist, yielding membrane of modern life.

It is also perhaps symbolic of Cheeser's well-documented flirtation with crime and punishment, in that there are definite penal undertones at play here. Raskolnikov himself would have recognized the essential elements of the prisoner's escape kit: a thin blade, with which to saw through bars, and a small chestnut, on which to gnaw as one made one's perilous way through the frozen steppes of Siberia. The use of the rubberized sheath is less clear in this reading, yet it appears to contain a message of hope and quite possibly rotund, ripening expectation.

Judge's comment:
'Was it Cheeser, or indeed, Biggus Dickus?'

TURNIP RATING:

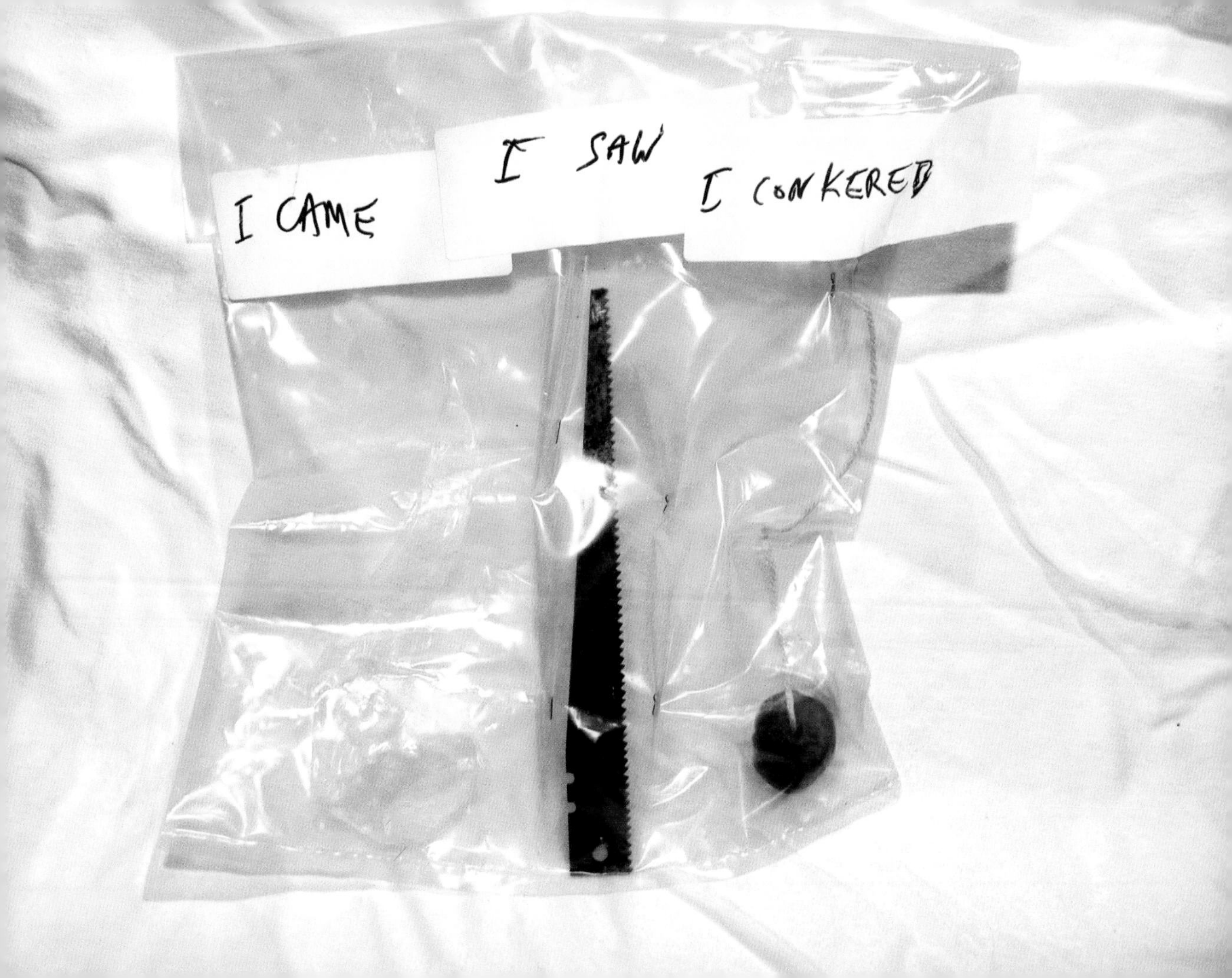
I CAME
I SAW
I CONKERED

IN T'NET PRAWN

BY IVOR BONER

2015, STRING, PORCELAIN, CRUSTACEAN

Grimsby-born, Eton-educated artist Ivor Boner once again harnessed the diversity of his background to produce a work for the 2015 competition that posits the comparative affluence of his later years against his poverty-stricken childhood.

Boner came from a fishing family and spent his early years picking coal on local beaches. Before his 12th birthday young Boner was beginning to be talked about in the (albeit limited) circles of regional-art agitators The Cleethorpes Movement for his unique 'dust art', created from remnants of meagre fires in the family hearth. A scholarship to Eton proved just the ticket, and Boner's work leapt exponentially in terms of its enduring sophistication. *To Hell with Hull*, a 1994 video installation that saw shop dummies dressed as his parents dragged along the M1 behind a 1936 racing-green open-topped Bentley (while Boner sat in the back, spitting vintage Champagne at them) made its debut at the Saatchi Gallery and was hailed as a *chef-d'oeuvre*.

In T'Net Prawn quite literally recaptures some of the flavour of those early responses. The deliberate use of common Northern vernacular in the title, the image of the prawn as a symbol of luxury snared by a net (representing Boner's upbringing): such disparate elements are magically woven together in an epistemological piece that leaves the viewer gasping for breath in much the same way as a haddock, freshly retrieved from the North Sea. The prawn itself seems to be rendered asunder, representing Boner's schism from his embarrassing Northern roots, and it is this dislocating isolationism that he continues to pursue artistically, for the entertainment and pleasure of art connoisseurs across the whole of the South of England.

Judge's comment:
'A damp squid of an entry.'

TURNIP RATING:

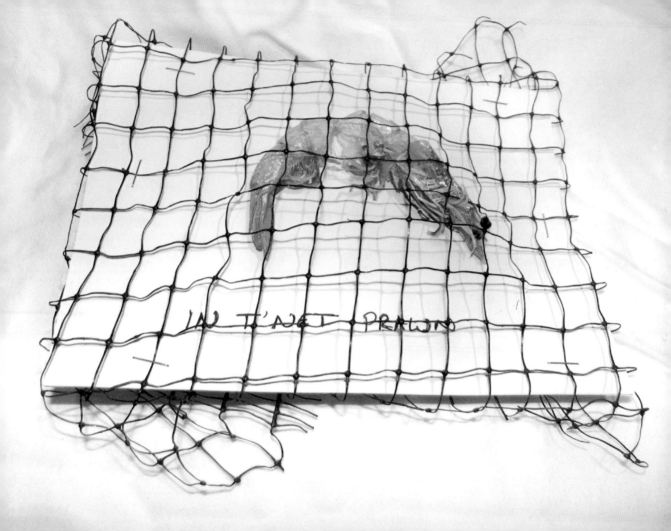

JAMMING WITH MUDDY WATERS

BY JIM DREW

2011, MUD, WATER, GLASS

'My art', wrote Richard Long, the celebrated British exponent of what has become known as Land Art, 'is the essence of my experience, not a representation of it.'

Long's 50 years in the field, making art from his own bodily movements (as it were), has heralded a growth – nay, an entire industry – in creating works from matter found on *terra firma*: earth, water, grass and shit. There are those who argue that the latter substance is a metaphor for all so-called 'Land Art'; this critic would not be among them, though it would be expedient to confess that while one might appreciate the extraction of fecal matter to inspire an artist, one doesn't necessarily want it on one's wall.

The essence of Long's 'experience' is distilled in *Jamming with Muddy Waters*, Jim Drew's profoundly spiritual response to the music of the great Blues legend. The combination of water and earth summons forth the experience of African slaves (from whom Waters was descended), snatched from sacred soil and transported across the oceans, hollering what later became the complete works of Eric Clapton as they sallied forth. The vessel in which they travelled is there in Drew's subtle use of the jam jar: an image of shelter and a repository for sustenance, usually jam.

Indeed, is this not the face of Mr Waters himself we see on the jar? The eyes scrunched tight and the mouth bewailing the fact that he got up this morning and his woman was gone suggest this is the case, and that Waters's own experiential essence has been fomented and found within its confines.

Judge's comment:
'Looks like shit to me.'

TURNIP RATING: 🐁🐀🐀🐀🐀

KNICKERLESS CAGE

BY SUE SHE

2009, TWISTED WIRE, MOULDED PLASTIC, FAKE HAIR

Stripped of their vestments, clawing at the wire, the trapped, smiling Barbies pander to their collective master – the unseen (yet undoubtedly priapic) Ken.

Sue She's *Knickerless Cage* is driven by an unseen, urgent male presence. For the iconic female inmates the world beyond the cage holds the promise of freedom. But only cooking, cleaning, knitting, reading groups and abject sexual servitude to Ken await.

Created in 2009 the revelatory work remains a *tour-de-force* commentary on metropolitan sexual politics. The artist asks us to confront the futility of women being perceived as anything other than sex objects. In their caged world the dolls will compete for supremacy; then for escape; then – viciously – for Ken's sexual favours.

The artist is smart enough to make references to 16th-century art pleasingly opaque, but this work is saturated with references to Lucas Cranach the Elder's *Venus with Cupid Stealing Honey* (1531), where a bee-stung Cupid is openly disrespected by an indifferent, sex-crazed Venus. *Knickerless Cage*'s reverse take on Cranach suggests these unfortunates are also going to be stung – not by bees, but by Ken.

It would be infantile to suggest that the title of this piece bears any reference to the Hollywood actor Nicolas Cage (*Leaving Las Vegas*, *Face/Off*, *Con Air*, *Left Behind*, etc.).

Judge's comment:
'Boobs and bums – and still complete bollocks.'

TURNIP RATING: 🐢🐢🐢🐢🐢

LIFE ON MARS

BY A. LIEN

2010, PLASTIC, CHOCOLATE REMNANTS

The death of David Bowie in early 2016 robbed the world of a major artistic talent: a creator who could flit between music, visual art, film, literature and dance. For this critic, 1967's 'The Laughing Gnome' is the apogee of his genius, showcasing the innate ability of the artist to mix media effortlessly while insouciantly presenting the whole as 'pure' entertainment. Others may disagree but I find them wrong.

But it is to the Seventies that we must turn for the ideological provenance of this piece, subtly referencing two distinct recorded works from the late artist: the 1971 single 'Life on Mars' and the album *The Rise and Fall of Ziggy Stardust and the Spiders from Mars*, released the following year.

Bowie's obsession with Mars bars substantially predates his celebrated Thin White Duke period of 1976 and his time of drastic weight loss. Here one finds a 'hungry' artist in all of the (rotund) senses of the word: an artist desperate for fame, an artist engorging three square meals in his diet. So it would be that 'The Man Who Fell to Earth' actually fell on Slough's finest-ever example of confectionery, finding solace, inspiration and comfort therein.

In this absurdly clever, provocative work of visual creativity, *Life on Mars*, A. Lien explores the dichotomy to devastating effect. Bowie, the spider, determinedly labours towards the torn opening in the wrapper, hoping to seek out and 'consume' inspirational fuel to further an inexorable rise to world fame.

'And what will he find there?' poses the artist. The answer, sadly, is an empty packet, forcing our spider-man to progress an allegorical quest for the fame and fortune that he would, ultimately, make all his own.

Judge's comment:
'The artist is no jean genius... time for a ch-ch-change of career.'

TURNIP RATING:

MELANCHOLY

BY JUST THE TWO OF US

2013, PLASTIC, FRUIT

The subject of melancholy in art is a rich and varied one. Indeed, the clichéd visual ideal of 'the Artist' is of a floppy-haired fop, lying languidly across a chaise longue as a large dose of laudanum runs through his veins and his heart breaks at the thought of the beautiful woman he has loved and lost. I spent my entire twenties looking and feeling this way, until my father told me to get up off the 'settee' (yes, he used that hideous term!) and find something called 'a proper job'.

A terrible bastard was he, and it is to my eternal credit that I ignored him and found my true calling in life. Nevertheless, the streak of melancholy that he painted me with persists to this day, and so I identify deeply with Just the Two of Us's treatise on a subject that has fascinated artists for many centuries.

I, like the obedient dog atop the main feature of the work, would do my father's bidding simply to please him, which of course I never could. Oft-times I could be seen running through the early-morning streets of Dagenham, a copy of the newly purchased *Daily Mirror* in my mouth. And yes, as I trotted home to my ungrateful parent, my facial expression was that of the poor, forlorn and sorrowful melon we see in the piece, roughly hewn yet almost unbearably poignant.

Melancholy is a work that makes me weep instantly, particularly when I view it in conjunction with John Dowland's haunting melody of 1596, 'Flow My Tears' (later interpreted superbly by the artist known as Sting). The year of this piece's creation, 2013, was a melancholy one indeed, for it marked the passing of my beloved Margaret Thatcher, and when I imagine her face imposed upon the anguished melon on the opposite page, my heart breaks afresh once more.

Judge's comment:
'Barking up the wrong melon.'

TURNIP RATING:

MELANCHOLY
BY

NAILSEA

BY DAVID SUMMERS-COOKE

2013, METAL

Nailsea, I am told, is a small town on the edge of Bristol. Semi-rural, it nonetheless contains a mélange of 1960s-built dwellings which, when constructed, gave weary urbanites fleeing the city a chance to experience something of a rural idyll.

Today, the opposite is true. Every morning, at the crack of dawn (so my new research assistant Horatio tells me), the descendants of those first proletarian pioneers step into their cars and join a serpentine queue of commuter traffic heading into Bristol. Patiently, they glance at their copies of the *Daily Mail* and listen to dreary local-radio presenters as they sit 'bumper-to-bumper', according to the expression. Such lives, dear readers, that are thankfully far from the ones we lead...

Nailsea, by David Summers-Cooke, provides us with an understated, yet nuanced picture of life in commuter hell. The volte-face of those suburbanites drawn back to the city as if by magnet is encapsulated in the sweeping curve of the bent nail; an internal, eternal rhythm that draws individual humans to collective groups, as eels to the Sargasso Sea. The nail itself references the first syllable of the town's moniker and is also highly symbolic of the rash of house-building that took place 50 years ago.

Horatio also tells me that a semi-famous musical ensemble called The Wurzels, a collective of illiterate, ruddy-cheeked farm labourers who lived under hayricks, and sang for cider and cheese, was formed in Nailsea. A *soupçon* of the local vernacular was apparently added to the rendition of their lyrics, giving form to ditties such as 'Thee's Got'n Where Thee Cassn't Back'n, Hassn't'?

Indeed.

Thankfully, *Nailsea* refrains from such vulgarity and, as such, manages to claw back what scraps of dignity remain among the artistic cognoscenti who still remain in the town, somehow avoiding the herd-like draw to the city upon their doorstep.

Judge's comment:
'The artist must have been hammered when he did this.'

TURNIP RATING:

NAILSEA

PHONE HACKING

BY ANDY ROBINSON

2013, MOBILE PHONE, IRONMONGERY

Our deep sympathies naturally went to Andy Robinson for the violent desecration of his 2012 Turnip entry *Mobile Phone and Poached Egg*, a stunning work of philosophical insight that, had it survived, would have fetched record sums at auction.

However, after a year of contemplation, Robinson returned in 2013 with a savage riposte to the kind of cultural vandal who, over the centuries, has shot, stabbed or even vomited on works by such luminaries as Rembrandt, da Vinci and Mondrian.

Phone Hacking takes the very attack that destroyed its predecessor, reworking and subverting it into an object of unutterable grace and beauty. The phone lies prostrate, as a patient etherized upon an operating table, while the crude saw inflicts the kind of damage upon it that desperate battlefield doctors imposed upon wounded men in conflicts ranging back to the Crimea and beyond. 'By this action,' the piece is saying, 'so you will be a whole man once more. Albeit without an "OK" button. Or, indeed, a signal of any kind.'

International interest in the initial desecration was matched, and exceeded, by that which greeted news of the creation of *Phone Hacking*. However, fluctuations in the Chinese art market in 2013 meant that the work failed to reach its reserve price of £2.75 at Bonhams, and according to Robinson the piece has been placed in a south London lock-up, awaiting a fate as yet undetermined.

No matter. The validity of the work still stands as a fightback against the kind of cultural desecration, physical or verbal, that we in the Art World face on a daily basis. But we are as resilient as the eponymous phone: you cut us, you hurt us – but when we bleed, we bleed for the love of art.

Judge's comment:
'If you can get a signal in Wedmore it will be the news of the world.'

TURNIP RATING:

Phone Hacking

PLAY ON WORDS
BY PERCY LONG-PRONG

2013, PAPER

Percy Long-Prong is the foremost artistic interpreter of the Bard's oeuvre, constructing a tense, flowing dynamism between text and creative response. His 1978 *Richard III* (a video of flat-capped Cockney characters Lambeth-walking into piles of dog mess) and its 2001 follow-up *The Merry Wives of Windsor* (a triptych made from corgi dogs, gin bottles and tax demands) created controversy and courted affection in equal parts.

This 2013 effort, investigating the effects of *Macbeth* on contemporary language, broke an enigmatic artistic silence, self-imposed in 2002, apparently as a response to the election of Rowan Williams as Archbishop of Canterbury. Williams's standing down from the post in December 2012 effectively ended Long-Prong's ten-year hermitage. *Play on Words* is the newest, most successful piece in a lengthy and illustrious career.

A very worthy addition to the Turnip catalogue of winners, *Play on Words* insouciantly challenges the notion of 'everyday' words and the general 21st-century dumbing-down of language we have all witnessed with growing despair. '*Oxford Everyday Dictionary*, I will lay Shakespeare upon thee,' Long-Prong appears to say, 'and by the very force of his quill, ye Bard will verily impregnate thee with many good things.'

The 2013 judges concluded that *Play on Words* was a piece of effortless construction, breezily tossing a literary hand grenade into a broth of verbiage, lassitude and a couple of other ingredients. As expected, the results of this scholarly blast reverberated around the ivory towers of 'Eng Lit' for months afterwards. A good thing, too, for it seems these blasted departments get all the best Education Ministry funding. Bloody disgrace, if you ask me.

Judge's comment:
'In this case, Bill Shakespeare equals BS.'

TURNIP RATING:

PLAY ON WORDS

POO TIN

BY UNKNOWN

2015, PAPER, METAL, FAECES

Of late, political art has fallen out of fashion, and one wonders, amid the dreadful retro-bunting and cutesy stencils that one is regularly forced to assess, where the descendants of George Grosz, Joseph Beuys and William Hogarth might now be. Certainly not in the fetid corridors of the New Cross Academy for Dubious Talent, that's for sure.

Therefore, one can only admire the wit, skill and audacity of Unknown, who bravely submitted *Poo Tin* for the 2015 competition. In a totalitarian twist worthy of Kafka himself, the GPO almost refused to handle this exhibit on the grounds that it contained a noxious substance that could prove dangerous to anyone coming into contact with it. However, freedom of expression thankfully prevailed.

Unknown portrays the President as a skull-and-crossbones-like image on the mainsail of a ship that appears to be heading into the uncharted waters of what might uncouthly be described as 'shit creek'. The unbranded tin containing the vile effluent symbolizes the utilitarian, faceless nightmare of Russia's experience in the Communist era. A terrible business all round.

Poo Tin represents all that is fearful about unrestrained capitalism and shows us up as morally devoid of humanity and no better than the banal contents of a metal container. A powerful work indeed and one I would welcome in my collection – under a hermetically sealed cloche, of course.

Judge's comment:
'One tin, and two shits.'

TURNIP RATING:

QUEEN'S PEACH

BY LADY MUCK

2011, FRUIT, GUMMED PAPER, METAL PINS

The appearance of food and drink in art – a commonly discernible trope over many centuries – satisfies both technical and metaphorical/allegorical aims of artists past and present. The former is obvious – fruit is jolly hard to paint – the latter not so, but, over time, fruits, vegetables and nuts have all been attributed various symbolic meanings, according to the cultural, religious and societal norms during the period of artistic creation. One need only consider the apple, a medieval byword for lust, forbidden passion and temptation, to divine the evolution of this metaphorical process. In later times, the depiction of foodstuffs, particularly fish and eggs, is seen as a hint at male and female genitalia, *à la* Frans Hals's *Merrymakers at Shrovetide* (1616–17).

Queen's Peach is both an exercise in allegory and subversion. Self-styled 'Arse-ist' Lady Muck invites us to consider whether the curvaceous attributes of the peach should be considered in regard to the Royal Posterior. Or is it a statement about possession, entitlement and privilege? The position of the postage stamp, as though covering an orifice, hints at the former, reinforced by the image of the stamp itself, which in turn suggests Jamie Reid's 1977 Situationist take on Her Majesty for the Sex Pistols' 'God Save the Queen' single cover. The appearance of pins attaching said stamp to said fruit reinforces the idea of a punk sensibility, subverting the old British joke that licking a stamp – the glue being on the reverse side of the image – is like licking the Queen's behind. If this *is* the case, then it is a filthy image and has nothing to recommend it.

Now, how about that knighthood?

Judge's comment:
'First-class crap.'

TURNIP RATING:

SEPP PLATTER

BY UNKNOWN

2015, FUNGI, POLYTHENE, METAL

The history of art as it relates to mushrooms is, admittedly, somewhat limited. There was a small crop of mid-Victorian works that tended to depict the famous red-and-white spotted fly agaric mushroom in proximity to prancing fairies. In the early 20th century, such fairies and their mushrooms appeared again, only to disappear almost as quickly underground until a resurgence in the late 1960s.

However, artists in this latter period tended not to portray mushrooms as such, but were heavily influenced by the effects of particular branches of fungi, in particular the notorious *Psilocybe semilanceata,* better known as the 'magic mushroom'. The hideous daubs that graced gallery walls and contemporary album covers during that period are enough to provoke a prolonged shudder, even now. It was a very good thing when the Sixties became the Seventies and dry sherry was reintroduced as the mind-alterant of choice for talented young artists.

And so to *Sepp Platter*, a worthwhile but flawed attempt to examine the role of the mushroom in early 21st-century society. The four examples evidently point to a spiritual cycle of decay,

death and regeneration common to many global cultures, though the polythene-sealed 'platter' is perhaps indicative of Man's desire to preserve himself far beyond his naturally allotted time on this planet. There is also the concept of unknown danger at play here; the idea of an inert object such as the mushroom being lethally poisonous is a frightening yet intriguing one, tugging anxiously at the blithe, dancing fairy in us all.

My biggest concern with this work is its title. The mushrooms used are not, in fact, 'ceps' (*Boletus edulis*). They are common-or-garden white mushrooms (*Agaricus bisporus*), of the type sold in supermarkets or by noisy Cockney types in street markets. This lack of research, I feel, lets the piece down badly; I do wish challenging young artists such as this would be just one step less ignorant than they obviously are!

Judge's comment:
'This artist should be kept in the dark and fed bullshit.'

TURNIP RATING:

STICK ANOTHER SHRIMP ON THE BARBIE

BY AUNT SPONGE

2014, GELATINOUS SWEETS, PLASTIC, SUPERGLUE

Unfortunately, this artist is of ambiguous gender, as clearly the whole context of the work – a tangential look at sexual politics underpinned by a retro-Thatcherite political treatise on the state of the British fishing industry – is posited on whether the artist is male or female.

My guess is that it is the creation of a member of the fairer sex, given the somewhat hysterical nature of the lady depicted. Her unkempt, Boudiccan hair and vacant look give rise to a feminist subtext, but what that is, I cannot ascertain. Certainly, there are significant visual indicators in every aspect of this contentious work, not least the terrible woodchip wallpaper behind our model. Has she thrown a mug of tea violently against it, before stripping naked and covering herself in artificial decapod crustaceans? Is this a statement bemoaning the objectification of women and the so-called WAG (wives and girlfriends) era?

Possibly yes, but I prefer the interpretation that it is a comment on European pisciculture and the limits thereof on our own domestic fishing fleet. 'The Europeans,' it suggests, 'with their ridiculous quotas and intrusions on sovereign waters, are sticking it to us. Quite literally.' Our splendid nude Venus throws up her hands as the foreigners hurl their catch at her breasts and genitals, shaming her into wild, abject surrender. As a riposte to the supposed feminist subtext, consider this vision of British womanhood in contrast to the box-like silhouette of German *Kaiserin* Angela Merkel, who, given the opportunity, would force *Deutsch*-speaking cod, haddock and plaice upon us all.

To borrow a phrase from our 'former' foes, *Stick Another Shrimp on the Barbie* is a *Zeitgenössische Kunst* statement of the highest order, and perhaps the lady who created it would like to make herself known, so that she may be presented with a lovely bouquet of flowers and a WH Smith voucher for her efforts.

Judge's comment:
'Fuck Ken Hell.'

TURNIP RATING:

STONE HE BROKE

BY HAROLD STONE

2012, STONE

The move away from hunting-gathering and towards farming is arguably one of the significant waypoints in Man's journey towards the Modern Age. No longer would our ancestors occupy roughly hewn stone structures or inseminate females of the tribe without a care for paternal loyalty – though some might argue that contemporary housing estates around Britain's ghastlier Northern towns and cities to this day engender the self-same approach to base survival. The domestication of both animals and women were important steps on the road to what we recognize today as society, leading directly to Man's consideration for himself as 'Artist', a soul whose plane soared far beyond that of the state we might call 'work'.

And so to *Stone He Broke*, by the aptly named Harold Stone. A lichen-covered pebble of indeterminate age, no doubt carefully selected from the myriad of similar examples to be found across Somerset, is split into unequal halves placed around one inch apart. The allegorical reference to nearby Cheddar Gorge is obvious. Less blatant, perhaps, is the violence with which the rock has been riven in two, suggesting Neolithic Man's sudden, decisive break with his primordial past, heralding a more progressive future.

The disfigurement of reality in order to create significant works of art is not always a modern concern – while one immediately thinks of Bacon's triptychs, we might also consider Holbein the Younger's majestical *The Ambassadors* (1533) and the extraordinary anamorphosis of the *memento mori* at the bottom of the frame. To pervert existing structures is not necessarily to cast aside their essential integrity; indeed, by destroying that which *is*, one necessarily creates a thing which *is not*. Or perhaps which *also* is. Except that it is not what it was. Or, indeed, is.

Judge's comment:
'Finding talent here is like trying to get blood out of a stone.'

TURNIP RATING:

THE ASHES

BY KAY PEA

2015, COAL, WOOD, METAL

Nothing whatsoever to do with international cricket and everything to do with a post-apocalyptic world, in which survivors must dig through the burnt remnants of hyper-capitalism, artist Kay Pea's *The Ashes* is highly redolent of the conceptual work of Yoko Ono. Indeed, had the word 'sniff' been written in the dust by a certain Liverpudlian's index finger, the provenance of this piece would not have been in question. According to Bonhams, such incontrovertible proof would have seen the artwork priced at somewhere around £1.3 million.

As it is, *The Ashes* is worth around 13 pence, roughly the rateable value one would pay the local council to take it away and dispose of it thoughtfully. Is it right, though, to put a price on such an enigmatic form? For while there is little intrinsic value, I feel the piece has a certain symphonic, redemptive quality; there are notes of shape-shifting movement beneath the remainders of the inferno that has destroyed mankind, and where carbon survives there is hope that life itself will one day regenerate.

The piece's most remarkable feature is the appearance of a small orange leaf just off-centre. Here, I feel Pea is hinting at a world that has experienced The Fall not once, but twice; the damaged leaf symbolizing Man's helplessness in the face of the impending climate crisis and the irreversible damage to the planet caused therein. If Pea continues to produce work of this quality, I feel she has a bright future in the art world – unless, of course, she is fried alive with the rest of humanity in a meteor strike…

Judge's comment:
'An artistic farewell; dust to dust, you might say.'

TURNIP RATING:

TOILET HUMOUR

BY N. EEDAL IFE

2012, PAPER, PORCELAIN

Toilet humour – where would we be without it, hmm? Well, we certainly wouldn't have made such strident advances in modern art, certainly, for it was a toilet that started off the whole idea of the everyday as an art object. In 1917, Marcel Duchamp famously signed a rather functional urinal with the moniker 'R. Mutt', entitled it *Fountain* and attempted to display it as a work of art at the Grand Central Palace in New York.

His attempt was thwarted by the ignorami, who somehow thought there were more fitting subjects for art (the ongoing First World War, perhaps) than an ordinary *pissotière*. However, common sense prevailed, and Duchamp's bog was eventually and quite rightly seen as one of the major artistic statements of the 20th century. Had it not been for *Fountain*, there would be no Turnip – or, indeed, Turner – Prize. And a sadder, quieter and more stupid world it would be.

Duchamp's intellectualization of the commonplace is echoed in *Toilet Humour* by renowned Arabian artist N. Eedal Ife. The concentric circles of inner and outer bowls contrast beautifully with *The Ultimate Dirty Joke Book*, balanced thrillingly on the part of the porcelain where the seat would usually be. Ife hints that anyone daring to use the toilet bowl for its proper function will be grossly disappointed, particularly those attempting bowel movements. Only cold clay awaits the behind; a hint, perhaps, of Man's reductive role as a mere food processor and the ultimate fate that awaits everyone, from king to commoner. Ife's is a thoughtful, perceptive piece and a tribute to those of us who are able to distinguish what art truly is, and what it is not, i.e. shit.

Judge's comment:
'Too clean; not shit enough by half.'

TURNIP RATING:

#@*%!#@*%! THE
ULTIMATE
DIRTY
JOKE
BOOK

Mike Oxbent
& Harry P. Ness

TOILET HUMOUR
by
N Eedal Ifie

TORN BEEF

BY IAN LEWIS

2006, FLESH, METAL

In 2006, bad manners, bad taste and bad people seemed to collide like a drunken conga to create some of the worst art of the new millennium – and we still have a few years of artistic hangover from those foolish, prelapsarian days.

However, there were some shining beacons during that period, and *Torn Beef*, a worthy Turnip Prize-winner in 2006, is proof of that. Artist Ian Lewis takes us back to the long-lost 1980s and specifically 1982 – the year of the Falklands conflict. If one casts one's mind back, a major concern then was that Our Boys might not get the tins of bully beef that have sustained the British Army since Waterloo, due to the Argentinians banning exports of the stuff to enemy territory. But, fortuitously, an SAS raid on a Mendoza canning factory ensured that around 275,000 tins were liberated, at the cost of no British lives.

Torn Beef celebrates this little-known action, which earned the regiment no less than seven VCs. The tin has evidently been bayoneted initially and the contents partly wolfed down. Then the hapless squaddie has discovered the key and liberated the rest of the meat by conventional means. An obscure white shape on the front of the tin is, on closer inspection, revealed to be a map of South America, with the so-called *Malvinas* appearing to float away from the mainland with an air of unflappable cool.

One is tempted to mention Henry Moore, who also created metal objects with holes poked in them, but I fear this may be something of a calumny; Lewis's work is a rather more antediluvian riposte to sculpture's enduring obsession with anything *au courant*. Indeed, despite the warlike nature of *Torn Beef* this is a far more quiescent piece. 'The world of corned beef', Lewis seems to note, 'has, after war, breathed relief.'

Lovely rhyming, don't you agree?

Judge's comment:
'Bull in a box.'

TURNIP RATING: 🐀🐀🐀🐀🐀

WICKED LEEKS

BY JULIE-ANNE STRANGE

2012, INK, VEGETABLE

I must admit, upon receipt of this work, to being somewhat baffled by it, for I could not see what might be intrinsically wicked about a pair of seemingly innocuous leeks. True, the faces scrawled upon them are of a 'low' type, but hardly Hitlerian. A raised eyebrow and a goatee beard of the type many of us sported in the hedonistic, duffel-coated days of The Slade and, later, Soho's Pretentious Gallery, do not monsters make; indeed, there is something rather lovable about these two rascals.

I searched high and low amid the treasures of the British Library to find some classical reference to vegetables having malign intentions but, alas, discovered nothing. Puzzled, I asked Phillipe, a pale, ravaged-looking youth at the New Cross Academy for Dubious Talent, what his opinion was. Pausing to wipe a section of crust-like matter from the side of his nose, he replied, 'Well, it ain't leeks, that's for sure. Nuffin' to do wiv 'em. It's "Wicked Leeds", innit?'

I asked him to explain, and he did. In the 1970s, it seems that the grim Northern city of Leeds sported an eponymous football team that had a reputation for foul play on the field.

The epithet given to this particular team was 'Dirty Leeds' – not, you will agree, a huge leap to 'Wicked Leeds'. Of course! Young Phillipe was correct! Oh, how my heart swelled as I referenced further and saw the grinning, unrepentant faces of such Leeds United luminaries as Norman 'Bites Yer Legs' Hunter, William 'Billy' Bremner and Johnny 'Johnny' Giles scrawled upon those very leeks.

With subtlety and sleight of hand, artist Julie-Anne Strange has outwitted the UK's most respected art critic and may I say *'Félicitations pour votre beau travail'* to her. And to dear Phillipe, too; surely one of my most outstanding students this year.

Judge's comment:
'The shittest piece of modern art this side of the Ecuadorean Embassy.'

TURNIP RATING:

HOW TO ENTER THE TURNIP PRIZE

1.

Think –
very hard –
of a subject.

2.

Create your artwork in
the worst way possible,
using no effort, skill
or talent.
Things that might help with
the creative process: make it
topical, create a pseudonym
and a pun, and finally ask
yourself, 'is it crap?'

3.

Send your pile of
appalling crap between 1st
and 21st November only to :

Turnip Prize
c/o The New Inn
Combe Batch
Wedmore
Somerset
BS28 4DU

4.

Sit back and wait to hear if
you are Britain's most crap
artist!

ACKNOWLEDGEMENTS

Trevor would like to thank Amanda for all her efforts in helping with the organizing and for doing the techno stuff to make this publication happen. Thanks to Timmsy for all the help and for forgetting the website password! Also thanks to The New Inn, Wedmore, for putting up with all the shit and, more importantly, thanks to all of the crap artists for entering and using the least amount of effort possible.

Royston Weeksz wishes to thank Charlie Viney, Jessie Mills and Hannah Knowles for their unwavering commitment to the ending of philistinism and general ignorance. Thanks also to La Melanie, for her muse-like qualities and *joie de vivre*.

It's not what you earn from art in life, it's the fun and enjoyment you have along the way...

An Hachette UK Company
www.hachette.co.uk

First published in Great Britain in 2016 by Cassell, a division of
Octopus Publishing Group Ltd
Carmelite House
50 Victoria Embankment
London EC4Y 0DZ
www.octopusbooks.co.uk

ISBN 978 1 84403 939 5

A CIP catalogue record for this book is available from the British Library.

Printed and bound in China.

10 9 8 7 6 5 4 3 2 1

Every effort has been made to contact the creators of the entries included in
this book where their identities were known.

Commissioning editor Hannah Knowles
Senior editor Pauline Bache
Copy editor Kate Moore
Creative director Jonathan Christie
Production controller Meskerem Berhane